Libraries
ReadLearnConn

THIS BOOK I
ISLINGTON F
SCHEME

Please take this book and either return it to a Bookswap site or replace with one of your own books that you would like to share.

If you enjoy this book, why not join your local Islington Library and borrow more like it for free?

Find out about our FREE e-book, e-audio, newspaper and magazine apps, activities for pre-school children and other services we have to offer at www.islington.gov.uk/libraries

monsoon

In the lap of the storm clouds—the rain comes—
Its hair loosened, its sari borders flying!

—RABINDRANATH TAGORE

monsoon

words
SUDEEP SEN

images
MAHMUD

www.sudeepsen.com
Copyright © Words by SUDEEP SEN 2002
Copyright © Images by MAHMUD 2002
Additional Photo by SIMON KAY © 2002 on pages 32-33 / 128

All rights reserved

Published by
BENGAL FOUNDATION
House 9B, Road 71, Gulshan-2, Dhaka
<bf@bdonline.com> <bf@citech-bd.com>
www.bengalfoundation.org

Available in the United Kingdom & India from
AARK ARTS BOOKS
65 Greenford Road, Harrow HA1 3QF. London
J-1889 Chittaranjan Park, New Delhi 110019
aarkarts@sudeepsen.com

No part of this book maybe used or repr oduced in any manner whatsoever
without the written permission of the author and publisher except
in the case of quotations embodied in critical articles or reviews.

British Library Cataloguing in Publication Data
Sen, Sudeep, 1964— / Mahmud 1961—
Monsoon
I. Title; II. Prose/Poetry; III. Photography
821'.9'14

ISBN 1-899179-10-0 [Aark Arts]

Copyright © First Edition by Bengal Foundation, 2002
Copyright © Concept & Choreography by SUDEEP SEN/Aark Arts 2002
Design & Computer Graphics by RAJIB AHSAN. <maskofrajib@hotmail.com>
Title Calligraphy ~monsoon~ by MAHMUD/Map © 2002
Typeset in Perpetua 11/15 pts.

First Edition

for
Priti, Aria & Sara
sudeep

for
my parents
mahmud

LIQUID CONTENTS

Banquo: *It will rain tonight.*

First Murderer: *Let it come down.*

   —WILLIAM SHAKESPEARE, *Macbeth,* (III.iv.24)

She faded, like a cloud which had outwept its rain.

   —PERCY BYSSHE SHELLEY, *Adonais*

The
FIRST OCTET

rain, maps

It has started raining—sharp shards of transparent sheets hit the glass of the window that threatens to crack, but upon meeting its surface, melt to water. There is a constant blur of water outside. It is a curiously inviting scene, one that seems misty with flickering crystals glowing in parallel striations—the patterns changing their tack depending on the wind's mood swings.

I look at this grand show of rain everyday and everyday I weave a different pattern, both due to my own mood and the weather's inherent currents. Each day I weave a little piece, adding a patchwork to this infinite quilt, one that buries unwanted narratives in the warmth and cosy of its apparent comfort.

The way the quilt's colour and imprint form are unpredictable. The only thing that is known is the exact square-inch space that each segment will add up to. Its individual design is unknown until it is stitched on to the larger stretch of linen. It is a journey, mapping a route that is largely undecided, perhaps even unknown.

I like this mystery. It allows one to completely imagine and plot a path that suits one's own sense of direction. I have a compass to find the Earth's cardinal points. But this is of no use when it comes to details of

terrain, temperature, vegetation, and the unexpected inhospitability of travel itself.

I like the unknown, the unpredictable, the sense of encountering the virgin, even though the path might have been traversed before. But I do not have that knowledge, so it is entirely fresh, untrammelled, and personal. I begin walking.

I can walk anywhere from almost anywhere. I do not need time tables, or ports of embarkation and disembarkation. I do not need guidance of the tourist trade, or the help of someone who has done it before. I just venture out; let my legs do the walking, my eyes do the seeing, and my heart do the navigating. And amid all this, my mind keeps me company, as I imagine, dream, and see—visual and virtual, spontaneous and sure.

languor, wet

A typical start to a Dhaka day, more like an extension of last evening. The quality of light is the same as yesterday's—deep grey with an immense cloud over-hang. The electric lights inside are still on, as though they weren't turned off last night. There is a heavy, brooding, damp quality in the air that seems to invisibly wrap my exposed skin. My hair feels humid—even the upholstery, the clothes, and the trapped house-air.

I step out into the back garden. The soil is clayish and waterlogged. The plants look prosperous and overgrown though the lack of sunshine today does not highlight the clarity of fresh green. The insects, caterpillars, and spiders are busily getting on with their business, entirely unperturbed.

Rashid, our guard and gardener, sits outside under the drive's front porch pondering what to do. He has a perennial uninterested look that transforms to a semi-bright spark whenever any of his employers are in sight. There is a lot he could do, but he does very little, blaming his inactivity on the weather.

rain, rain

It is another space, another view, but the same rain. It has been raining all of last night through to this morning. It changed to a drizzle for about twenty minutes before resuming its full fury. But in its fury, there is an overbearing sense of surety and steadiness of intention. There is a constancy with which the water pelts down the striated streams of liquid.

It is hot and muggy, though clear—one of those slow languorous days, deceptive because it looks hopeful and bright at the outset, but the moment one attempts to do anything, it starts raining and a heavy soporific lull sets in.

———

fern frost

In front of my desk, the glass panes on the window are frosted—but the temperature inside is not freezing. Outside, the tropical pre-rain humid-heat of the afternoon makes the sight of broad-leafed palm trees an epitome of brooding languor, and plenitude.

The air in my study is cool, perhaps even conditioned cold, relative to the heat outside. Plain acts of physics and geometry make simple sights alter their guise; change from one state to another, even though that may be transitory.

There are definite mathematical equations to corroborate such sights, well-tested algorithms—but for me, illusions provide more room for imagination than the exact state of space.

The palm leaves outside are huge, enormous, like large fern-sails, their edges defined by the crisp 'cut-n-stitch' along their invisible seams. Their strength and dignity must come from the elegance of their trained spine.

All this is much like the gaze of a sophisticated onlooker—a visualiser—who sees the same scene with a different sense of calm, poise, thought, and imagination.

air-conditioner, rain

Isolated amid the air-conditioned comfort, vast well-cleaned concrete spaces, and the shelter of tropical profusion, I feel completely cut off from the hustle and bustle of metropolitan living I have been used to for decades.

It is cold in this room. The temperature belies the climate of the external topography and terrain. It is this chill that keeps me awake, otherwise the dull humidity of the outside's dead heat induces an infectious sleep.

It is raining again, but today's is a beautiful kind of rain—steady, symmetrical, confident, and unobtrusive. It has a kind of presence that is omnipresent without actually announcing that it is there, like 'ambient' music, though that would be too cruel a comparison. Somehow technological similes used to compare elements in nature are always fraught with dubious results.

I work here having lost the sense of time and its own presence of metre. Somehow natural syllabics have their own quiet momentum, one that leads you forward, setting their own pace and mapping their own space, much like the process of breathing itself.

Natural breath pace and its pauses have always been crucial to my own sense of textual pacing, the way they wind and twist displaying their curious unpredictable intentions.

heavy metal

Ship-breakers, snake-like in a single-file, slither towards monumental vessels stuck aground in the rain-swept muddy delta. This is Chittagong's heavy-metal graveyard, where abandoned big queens of the high seas are left to reminisce about their past glamour and glory.

Most of these workers are day-labourers—each, like a foot-soldier in an ant march, is an emaciated cog in the giant flesh-and-metal machinery—most of them

untrained in dismantling thick sheets of steel. Their
mud-coloured bodies glisten, as their gleaming sweat
and the acrid water's viscous reflection in the marsh-
pool threaten to boil over in the sun.

But there is hope—hope for a colony of people
earning a temporary meagre living—hope for the
virgin soil to mingle with the poisoned rust of the
ships so that both can learn the effect of
contamination—and hope too for an onlooker for
images that propel creativity.

The ships stand, rain-soaked, statuesque in spite of
their exposed dismantled skeletons. Bit by bit, they
will be further broken down and sold for scrap metal,
and many of their fixtures will be sold as display items
in brass and antique shops in the big cities.

Scrap metal never held such fascination and beauty in my eyes before. In spite of this wet panorama's unconventional composition—the scene somehow had a haunting quality of expansiveness that defied the obvious imagery of labour, extortion, and death.

~

monsoon greens

Green is the colour most visible to me these
days—glazed-oil green, light-banana green, olive
green, dry green—the green myopia of politicians;
the green armoury of warfare, the green under-
growth—all twisted and weed-like, green and
unstable, and no one in sight to prune or train them.

Shades of verdure had caused a blinding effect on my
system. Trendy herbalists are wrong—instead of a

soothing, calming effect, green has a peculiarly vulnerable, nausea-inducing effect on me.

Green bile and vomit, a Frankenstein-fantasia, green-mucous cough spat by tuberculosis patients, green moss and grime in unclean toilets and storm-drain ditches that line the roads—beautiful green, awful green, healthy green, wet green, monsoon green.

Monsoon has arrived—persistent in intent, green in jealousy. The rain is going to be around for a while, only hastening and never dampening the insidious, monochromatic, chameleon-spread of green.

bengal rain

Rain has sparked so many imaginations all over the world. But there is nothing like the rain in the two Bengals—West Bengal in India, and Bangladesh.

Rain in its overbearing gait, its preparation, its stature, its brooding quality, and its romantic heavy-lidded cloud structure. Ordinarily one would call these rain clouds 'cumulonimbus', but that name or model does not in any way do them justice.

Here the clouds assume a deep grey-black quality, and just prior to a heavy downpour it is almost pitch-dark. The leaves rustle around in little circular flurries, there is a pregnant heaviness in the air, the smell of wet clay and the hustling sounds of birds taking shelter permeate the sky.

Barsha, as the monsoon rains are locally known, has a truly unmatchable resonance—elegant, weighty, ponderous, raw, but always striking and graceful.

It was not raining rain to me,

It's raining violets.

—ROBERT LOVEMAN (1864-1923), 'April Rain'

rain / came down in slanting lines

—ALEXANDER SMITH (1830-1867), *A Life Drama*

The
SECOND OCTET

rain charm

Another rain-swept day leaves everything water-logged—ponds, drains, streets, and rivers—everywhere water is overflowing. The green blades of grass in the garden lie submerged under a rippling shallow sheet of water. Through refraction, they take on magical underwater seaweed shapes. Except here, the grass is evenly cropped, so it appears as a glazed woven mat of wet-green. Rain has also left the plants and trees gleaming, bursting in plenitude.

Natural irrigation in excess creates its own slow rot, a sublime slime of wet decay and birth, profusion and irresistibility. Rain has this special seductive appeal—its innocuous wet, its piercing strength, its gentle drizzle-caresses, its ability to douse and arouse. The entire charm lies in its simplicity.

raining rain

rain rain rain rain rain rain rain rain rain rain rain rain
rain rain rain rain rain rain rain rain rain rain rain rain
rain rain rain rain rain rain rain rain rain rain rain rain
rain rain rain rain rain rain rain rain rain rain rain rain
rain rain rain rain rain rain rain rain rain rain rain rain

rain rain rain rain rain rain rain rain rain rain rain rain
rain rain rain rain rain rain rain rain rain rain rain rain
rain rain rain rain rain rain rain rain rain rain rain rain
rain rain rain rain rain rain rain rain rain rain rain rain
rain rain rain rain rain rain rain rain rain rain rain rain

rain rain rain rain rain rain rain rain rain rain rain rain
rain rain rain rain rain rain rain rain rain rain rain rain
rain rain rain rain rain rain rain rain rain rain rain rain
rain rain rain rain rain rain rain rain rain rain rain rain
rain rain rain rain rain rain rain rain rain rain rain rain

rain rain rain rain rain rain rain rain rain rain rain rain
rain rain rain rain rain rain rain rain rain rain rain rain
rain rain rain rain *raining violets* rain rain rain rain rain
rain rain rain rain rain rain rain rain rain rain rain rain
rain rain rain rain rain rain rain rain rain rain rain rain

rain rain rain rain rain rain rain rain rain rain rain rain
rain rain rain rain rain rain rain rain rain rain rain rain
rain rain rain rain rain rain rain rain rain rain rain rain
rain rain rain rain rain rain rain rain rain rain rain rain
rain rain rain rain rain rain rain rain rain rain rain rain

night rain

I woke up at 3 a.m. with a start. I was shivering and sweating profusely at the same time. The cotton tee-shirt I had on was completely drenched. So was the bed-sheet I was lying on.

Outside I could hear the rain hitting the terrace floor with relentless ferocity. Thunder-claps shook the glass panes to near breaking point.

I love the sound of water and rain whatever their mood. It has a certain sense of assurance, a steadiness that isn't always present in the other elements.

I had a spontaneous desire to step out into the rain. I was drenched anyway, so getting the rain's feel on my back would do me no harm. Besides, getting wet in the night rain has its peculiar thrills.

I stepped out—my body heat met the rain. The rain-water sizzled off my skin steaming up in curls of white vapour.

All I could see and imagine was a blanket of hoar frost that enveloped me and the rain. Night rain camouflaged in the steam of body heat.

longing, rain

The very last drop of rain perched on the edge of her navel—the last bead of sweat balanced on the feather of her eye lash—

the last long-wet of my kiss on her skin—all these demand more, more, more—more wet, more wet—

yearning for more rain, fire, desire, moisture—and the cool chill of crystal-water, thirst, saliva, longing, rain.

shower, wake

The September showers came too late, giving ample
time for a prolonged drought. But when they
eventually arrived, they brought with them the full
fury of an unstoppered monsoon—the rain pelting
down hard, cracking open newly-laid tarmac,
exposing the earth and the elements once again.

The pouring water persisted, overflowing until
everything was effected—weak roofs, power lines,
trees, unwarned people, shelters—almost everything.

After two weeks, the storm subsided—a war-struck wet wake lay shattered in the aftermath, hungry, heavy, and low like polluted clouds of mist over a submerged *mofussil* that was trying to breathe and periscope back.

But here, the arteries are severed too severely to recoup their strength anytime soon. With or without water, in flood or drought, existence here remains unchanged.

rain, desire

The heavy sediment of Puerto Rican espresso sinks—in a deliberate silent-slow-motion thud—to the bottom of my glass mug. My head is infused in swirling aromatic fumes that wrap the morning's fresh-green rains. Moisture's deep taste defies my body's intention to stay dry.

It is cloudy—deep grey and about-to-burst—they over-hang teasingly, arching their backs, pregnant with wet's many-prismed face—merely seconds short of relief.

Everything around is still dry, though the damp's constant warning makes me wait—tentative, unsure when the cloud burst would release all its heat.

But imagining the rains can be far better than relentless rain itself. At least one can control its intensity of downpour, wind, force—imagine its desire, definition, and direction.

want, eager

Summer's dead heat—humidity teasing the clouds to shed rain—absolute stillness—every leaf balanced, though quivering, tentative—eager to feel the moisture on their skin.

~

offering, fluids

The kindness of libation, lyric, and blood. Her endless
notes left for me——little secrets, graces, trills
recorded on blue and purple parchment to be lipped,
tasted, devoured——only the essence remains, its
stickiness, its juice, its memory——

Seamless juxtaposition——the brute and the passion,
dry of the bone and wet of the sea, coarseness of the
page and smooth of the nib's iridium——

I try to trace a line, a very long line——the ink blots as
this line's linear edge dissolves and frays——like

capillary threads gone mad, twirling in the deep heat
of the tropics—threads unravelling, each sinew tense
with the want of moisture and the other's flesh.

There are no endings here—only beginnings—
precious incipience—translucent drops of sweat
perched precariously on her collarbone, waiting to
slide, roll unannounced into the gulleys that yearn to
soak in the rain—

Heartbeats shift the shape of globules as they alter
their balance and colour, changing their very point of
gravity—constantly deceiving the other—

I stand, wanting—wanting more of the bone's dry
edge, the infinite blur of desire, the dream, the wet,
the salt, the ink, the rain, and, the underside of her
skin.

It is perseverance that makes the difference
between seduction and courtship.
  —THE I CHING

The more you know, the less you need.
  —AUSTRALIAN ABORIGINAL SAYING

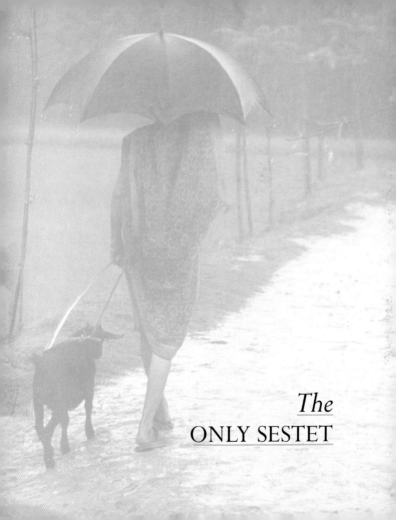

The
ONLY SESTET

morning, rain

Buried deep in warm skin—toasted in the night's long
passion, I struggle this morning—to emerge out of
this heavy, rain-filled air.

rain, kiss

A languorous kiss—the faintest smell of rain and ocean—salt-lipped breeze, pleading—

release, rain

The stamen raises its head—bursting, to shed pollen—relief-rain showers—the parched folds of pink skin.

<u>drizzle</u>, <u>climax</u>

Lips of a rose-bud open—to let the dew drop in—

drought, cloud

It is bone-dry—I pray for any moisture that might fall
from the emaciated skies—

There is a cloud, just a solitary cloud wafting
perilously—

But it is too far in the distance for any real hope—
for rain.

knowledge, need

"The more you know, the less you need"—but that is
not true at all for thirst, water, or rain.

~

COLOPHON

thank you

Our thanks to Simon Kay of The British Council for letting us use his photo that inspired the early version of the 'Heavy Metal' piece; to Fakrul Alam for the English translation of the Tagore couplet that appears on the frontispiece; to Kaiser Haq, Firdous Azim and Polly Gilbert for their editorial eye; to Rajib Ahsan for his help with computer layout & design input; to Sujan for scanning the images; to Sumon Beg, Jamil and Latif for hardware support, Moon and Reepon for other help; to Michiko for her invisible help; to Abul Khair Litu and Luva Nahid Chowdhury of The Bengal Foundation for project support; and most of all, to Priti & Aria for providing the inevitable sense of calm.

—S.S. & M.

acknowledgements

Many of the individual pieces in this book, some in earlier versions and under different titles, appeared in the following magazines, newspapers, journals, books, and the Internet. My thanks to the editors and publishers in the UK, USA, India, and Bangladesh who first commissioned and published them. They include:

Independent, Observer, Daily Star, Six Seasons Review, Aark Arts Review, British Council Quarterly, Literary Review, London Magazine, The Little Magazine, and in the following books:

Re-Imagining India: The Inlaks Anthology of Writing. Edited by Dr Niraja Gopal Jayal (Penguin, 2002);

Postcards from Bangladesh by Sudeep Sen, Tanvir, and Kelley Lynch (UPL, 2002);

Perpetual Diary by Sudeep Sen, Tanvir, and Kelley Lynch (Aark Arts, 2001); and

Lines of Desire by Sudeep Sen (USC, 2000).

–S.S.

type

This book is set in Perpetua—a typeface designed by the English artist Eric Gill, and cut by the Monotype Corporation between 1928 and 1930. Perpetua is a contemporary face of original design, without any direct historical antecedents. The shapes of roman letters are derived from the techniques of stonecutting. The larger display sizes are extremely elegant and form a most distinguished series of inscription letters.

musicware

Days of the Future Passed—The Moody Blues; *Solos, Duets and Trios*—Duke Ellington; *The Glimpse*—Trilok Gurtu; *Seal*—Seal; Fleetwood Mac; The Doors; Sting; Pink Floyd; Jethro Tull; *The Look of Love & Love Scenes*—Diana Krall; *Blues*—Eric Clapton; *Riding with the King*—B B King & Eric Clapton; *Emergency on Planet Earth*—Jamiroquai; *K & D Sessions*—Kruder & Dorfmeister; *Sahra*—Cheb Khaled; Stan Getz; Patricia Kaas; Kishori Amonkar; Hariprasad Chaurasia; Pandit Jasraj, *Making Music & Digha Rhythm Band*—Zakir Hussain; *Natural Elements*—Shakti; *Global Village*—Tor Dietrichson; *Conversations*—Stefan Grappelli & L Subramanium; and numerous Rabindra *sangeet* & Nazrul *geeti*.

hardware

Apple Macintosh G4 / IBM PC Pentium 4 / 1.3G /1.7G; P&A
Precision Colour LCD Flat Screen Display / 15.1; HDD 40 GB
Maxtor 7200 / 100; RR-DRAM 64 X 2 / 128; RDD 1.44 MB
Teac; Fax Modem 56K Aztech; Intel D850 Chip; VGA GeForce
2MX SHPRO; DVD ROM 12X Asus; CD-RW Samsung 12-8-32;
PS/2 Scroll Genius; P&A Multimedia; P&A Speakers 500 Watt;
Sound Creative 5.1 Live Box; Scanner Nikon LS-2000 & UMAX
1100, Hewlett Packard LaserJet 4P.

software

Microsoft Word, Adobe Photoshop, Adobe Illustrator, Quark
XPress, Adobe Acrobat, Eudora.

photoware

Nikon FM2 Camera; Nikkor Lenses——24mm, 28mm, 35mm,
105mm & 180 mm; Kodak Tri-X 400 ASA Film; Ilford
Photographic Paper.

books & chapbooks by sudeep sen

Poetry/Prose

Leaning Against the Lamppost

The Lunar Visitations

Kali in Ottava Rima

New York Times

Parallel: Selected Poems

South African Woodcut

Mount Vesuvius in Eight Frames

Dali's Twisted Hands

Postmarked India: New & Selected Poems

Body Text

Retracing American Contours

Almanac

Lines of Desire

A Blank Letter

Perpetual Diary

Postcards from Bangladesh

Monsoon

Editor/Translator

Lines Review Twelve Modern Young Indian Poets

Wasafiri Contemporary Writing from India, South Asia &
    The Diaspora

Index on Censorship Songs [Poems] of Partition

The British Council Book of Emerging English Poets
    from Bangladesh

In Another Tongue

Hayat Saif: Selected Poems

Love & Other Poems by Aminur Rahman

Aark Arts Review

Six Seasons Review

books by mahmud

As Photographer

Our World: Women in Bangladesh

Monsoon

the author

SUDEEP SEN [www.sudeepsen.com] was born in New Delhi in 1964 and studied literature there and the USA. As an Inlaks Scholar, he completed an MS from the Graduate School of Journalism at Columbia University in New York. He has written and edited over 20 books, including *Postmarked India: New & Selected Poems* (HarperCollins), which was awarded the Hawthornden Fellowship (UK) and nominated for a Pushcart Prize (USA). Most recently he has published *Postcards from Bangladesh* (UPL).

Sen has read his work world wide, won numerous awards, and published in leading publications such as the *Times Literary Supplement, Guardian, Independent, Financial Times, Evening Standard, London Magazine, Harvard Review, Times of India, Outlook, Biblio,* among many others. He has been an international poet-in-residence at The Scottish Poetry Library in Edinburgh and a visiting scholar at Harvard University. Sen works in publishing as an editorial director in London & New Delhi, and is an editor for *The Journal of Commonwealth Literature,* and *Six Seasons Review.*

the photographer

MAHMUD was born in Assam in 1961, but grew up in Dhaka. He co-founded Map, the first cooperative photo agency in Bangladesh, of which he is still an integral member. *Our World: Women in Bangladesh*, a wide-format book of black and white photographs, was published in Dhaka in 2000.

Monsoon is his second book of photographs to accompany the creative text of Sudeep Sen. Mahmud divides his time between Bangladesh and Nepal.

publisher's note

The delicate poetic fiction of Sudeep Sen and the photographic acumen of Mahmud have come together wonderfully in *Monsoon*. This project is an investment of their own individual skills——an artistic consummation that reinforces each other's [and our] vision of humanity, literature, and art. It is also an assertion of the dynamism of original thought, exchange of creative ideas—— something that adds an indelible value beyond the regular norms of exchange across borders and across disciplines.

In *Monsoon*, two Bengalis from the two Bengals, across two countries have powerfully created much more with their beautifully quiet and controlled gestures, than what is achieved through politics and clever diplomacy.

The monsoon rains in Bengal could only be what it is in its uniqueness——in Sudeep's words "elegant, weighty, ponderous, raw, but always striking and graceful"——coupled with its *yin-yang* ability to "douse and arouse". All these are a far cry from the frivolous and elusive Bashanta afternoons, *kodom, rimjhim*, deluged paddy fields, and other often-recorded hackneyed sights and sounds of this region.

We effusively present this book to our readers, our launch title in book-publishing——adding to our already various ventures in fine arts and music. *Monsoon* is a eulogy, a panegyric, a series of meditations, that inspires our role as a sustainer of the arts.

 BENGAL FOUNDATION

125

*Beauty of style and harmony and grace
and good rhythm depend on simplicity.*
—PLATO